the Art
of
BEING

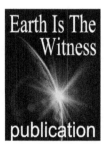
Earth Is The
Witness

publication

100 practices
to inner peace

the Art
of
BEING

the Joy of Living

an ultimate spiritual guide

Petar Umiljanovic

Earth Is The Witness publication

ISBN 9798385502387

Cover design by
Petar Umiljanovic

Earth Is The Witness

This is my Intellect
my Heart & Soul

speaking to You
in words of
Infinite Consciousness

my endless Love
for this World

for You

As You read it through

it will reward You
being forever written in
the Universe's Book of Life

I LOVE YOU

Contents

the Art of BEING

Mind

Consciousness

BEING

the Joy of Living

Loving

Spirituality

I N T R O D U C T I O N

Welcome, Dear Reader!

So we meet again, and this time
we'll keep it short as we slowly, profoundly
delve deep into our innermost being.

In this book, I will share simple yet awakening
wisdom to induce a state of full relaxation, peace,
and complete attentiveness to the now.

This is an absolutely beautiful collection of liberating messages divulged in timeless sets of instructions
that promise to move, enlighten and guide you to
feeling the power and pull of each moment.

Beingness is my favourite subject, and you will learn a lot about it in this booklet on the awakened self.

In its two chapters, you will learn about Being and Living; the Art of BEING and the Joy of Living; Beingness and Aliveness.

Each individual text will proffers a certain practice, which is typically indicated by its title or has been open for you to feel, interpret and internalise its meaning within yourself through the poem's pointers.

These new teachings are written in a consistent literate metre, in sets of three verses comprised of four lines, making them easy to follow and enjoyable to read. In the same spirit as the ancient Sutras, riddles, haiku, poetry, psalms, Sanskrit texts and Tao Te Ching, I invite you to embrace the opportunity to surrender to the absorption of the bliss you will find within these pages.

Together, we are destined to share the beauty of our inner being, to spread the knowledge of how to access the innermost wisdom of the true self, to fulfil humanity's promised liberation and purpose on this green and blue earth.

I fully and whole-heartedly invite You
to join me in this adventure of the spirit,
ignited by a flame of tasted bliss that is
flourish on the fires of enlightened awareness.

"Those who know don't talk,
and those who talk don't know.

Truth is never flashy;
fancy words are rarely true.

You don't have to leave your room
to grasp what's going on in the world;
nor do you have to look out the window
to appreciate the intricacy of the cosmos.

The further you roam, the less you see.

True Masters of The Light don't run around,
they see; they know.

They don't just look, they understand,
They don't do anything and
yet The Work gets done."

Chapter I

the Art
of
BEING

Mind

I Know

I know it is hard, well, unbearable,
so I know that you suffer, constantly,
I know you can't see the end of it, as the
eternity of painful feelings torment like suicide.

You have tried many things, been on countless trips,
with both your mind & feet, which brought you all
the pleasure of the experience, but what was the point
of breaking down walls while gaining no sense?

Have you not been listening, have you not been
warned, that by abusing the law of attraction you
will lose your soul, for it is you who shouts
loudest that breaks the flow of source.

Humble

You are not humble, you are not meek, but
you are sanctimonious, ain't that unique, to
be holier than thou, a self-righteous freak, no
humbling of ego, you'll always have to speak.

To be humble doesn't mean to not be proud,
because to be proud is to allow your natural
joy of being, sharing it freely is to be humble,
to help others and so proud of you they will be.

Of your good deeds don't take heed, don't write
a list, for in the moment of utmost dedication to
a fellow human, you're stripped of fear,
the prize is authenticity, while the price is peace.

No Resistance

If you really want to know the secret,
to open the holy grail of inner knowledge,
then listen to me, listen to those who have
done it already fully and wholeheartedly.

If you really want to succeed in achieving
abundance by finding peace and happiness,
then listen, as thus far, you have been failing
to acquire the means to being via solitude.

For what worth is there in forcing your way or
gathering fortunes, if you break their hearts by
losing yours for isn't it only by virtue of stillness
that one becomes present and non-resistant?

Depression

This powerful state has nothing at all to do
with being weak but with being too strong,
reaching the limit that the psyche can cope with
concerning its familiarity with the taste of freedom.

For this reason, non-dual understanding is
crucial in relaxing any efforts of trying to be
a person with a heavy story in the
world, instead, just being.

If you are really honest
you will be depressed,
if you stay still, there
is no polarised you.

No Despair

When all other lights have dimmed,
when all other paths have failed,
when all the people have left,
when only silence remains.

Then don't lose your mind,
don't hit your head, don't break your heart yet,
for this is your best chance, as you have been
given the keys to the universe itself.

You will soon find out for yourself that
tHere is only ever one door here, only one path,
one way, so now sit in silent presence, tranquil
in the knowing of your inner being.

Confidence

Are you going through life without a tale to tell,
bumping your head against everything,
taking wrong turns on mistaken paths,
without a conscious or clear way ahead?

Do you lack encouragement in making the
right decisions, do you feel lost or broken by betrayal,
or have people used you to better their own gains,
are you deficient in spiritual confidence?

If so, you are a truly lucky human, for your
absence has given many lifelong lessons that they
will learn sooner or later, but, from now on, you will
do everything with the confidence of consciousness.

Heart

Stop running from affection, stop fighting
the fear of brokenness, hiding like Rosicrucian,
building a wall around your well-being,
trembling from the persecution of inquisition.

Look at your loved ones, go give them a hug,
go give them a kiss, ask them how are they doing,
listen intently, tell them how proud you are
and tell them how much you love them.

Once you start acting from the highest joy,
sharing the deepest self and your freed love,
you will be centred in the heart,
in heart-centred consciousness.

Be the Light

How many lies you have been sold, how
many times have you been robbed of your soul,
you know there must be something disturbing
in the man, it must be his mindless vigilance.

If that's what prompts a man into acting senseless,
it therefore must be blamed on his unconsciousness,
but there is no prize in causing pain for shame's sake,
as only acts of endless love can resolve his problems.

You are the light of this world Jesus said, as you
can remain present in the face of abstinence,
this is your greatest gift and challenge,
to be the guide for those who stumble.

Reactions

You are the present being,
the knowing of experience,
observing what is appearing
within this stream of inner seeing.

What reaction does the world invoke
in you, which emotion does it conjure up,
which instinct drives you away from being
and remaining unmoved in stillness?

Notice any and all movement of thought,
that feelings or urges outlast by remaining
present and observant, they are but a slight
disturbance on the ocean of beingness.

Thoughts

You have these movements of consciousness
in order to distinguish between the two,
observing and establishing as the knowing
and realise your own lasting truth.

Your personality is a construct of thoughts,
an identity based on separate senses,
but you are the awareness of them, and
they will serve you if you allow them to be.

A thought is a tool, guidance to help you
interact and navigate in the apparent reality,
so observe your thoughts without attaching to them,
use them wisely, but don't forget to let them go.

Emotions

They make you feel vibrant and alive
don't they, so difficult to ignore them,
the very fact that you feel them
implies they are already identified.

But let them sway you, beautifully,
let them take you on the journey of
self-discovery through the feelings
they bring and the lessons they teach.

Awaken the soul by allowing yourself to
feel whatever shade they colour you in, for they
are the passions of life itself, whether sad or happy,
they swing then settle you in a middle way.

Sharpness

Don't be discouraged by its negative connotations, but know it for yourself as the Zen way of clarity, meaning to be precise, focused, determined, trustworthy, truthful, strong and sharp.

Practice an enlightened discipline and you are guaranteed to remain in the clearest state of constant intellectual, divine and humble worthiness, akin to a Shaolin monk, perceiving directly from beingness.

Then you can endure extremes of mind, such as suffering in loneliness, and extremes of weather, such as searing heat or bone-chilling cold, as you learn to remain fully relaxed in this concentrated sharpness.

Ambiguity

Be fearless in pursuing your destined career,
be absolutely free to express your opinion,
be completely relaxed about changing your stance,
contradict yourself most often, be ambiguous.

Allow yourself the privilege of being misunderstood,
don't stick to one idea, don't cling to the same
lifestyle, since existence can manifest in myriads of
states and forms, why experience just one or a few?

Represent variety, present diversity, offer multiple
choices to anyone who encounters you, create
numerous opportunities for everyone who crosses
your way, be clear in your many interpretations.

Polarity

Don't be afraid of taking sides to experience
opposites or different types of polarity,
don't hesitate to put yourself through many
extremes of experience to learn about duality.

The universe is an interplay of polarity, the yin-yang
type of reality that comes in the form of light & dark,
visible & invisible, male & female, love & hate,
positive & negative, life & death, big & small.

All of these dimensions of perception are here
by chance or by design, both are magnificent,
and by experiencing these polarities they
will establish your being in their midst.

Neutrality

The opposite of polarity is neutrality,
the decisive position to abstain from choosing,
the willingness to entertain peace and stability,
which is often much harder than taking sides.

To remain neutral is to forgo rushing things,
to assert the situation first and linger, waiting
for a better chance, to remain motionless,
to rest while others are restless.

It is your centre of the universe, your peace,
your awakened consciousness, your bliss,
it doesn't mean you are unable to make
a decision, it means you don't have to.

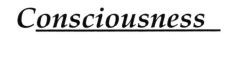

Consciousness

Here and Now

Is tHere anywhere else you could be,
is tHere any other place you can go to,
isn't this the only space that ever is,
how can we be everywhere and here?

Is tHere any other time you could be in,
is tHere anything else that isn't this space,
for how long do you think being out there
when the only time you could be is in the now?

How many thoughts are needed to settle you here,
how many places do you have to see to remain here,
how many times does it require to be in the now,
for how long will you evade the pure present?

Awareness

Why kept running away from yourself,
inevitably losing the opportunity to finally
catch up with stillness and find some peace
that has been waiting for the return of the self?

You are consciousness, the presence as awareness,
carrying your inner light forever inside, but to light
it up requires patience and perseverance,
concentration and observance.

Nothing outside of you will ever bare the fate
of your recognition as the self, only the inside can,
your serene peace in that perfect moment of
stillness is the only brunt by which to abide.

Mindfulness

How often do you see yourself in the mirror
and inquire about your trustworthiness
before you end up making a wrong turn
to find yourself in a mind-storm wilderness?

Those who do self-inquire into their own depths
will find moments of peace and happiness, and
by observing the voice of their false sense of self,
they are a step closer to breaking the mind-spell.

Surrender the ego to your internal hearing aid,
complete the search by wanting nothing more from
the system game, be present in the absorption of
stillness, always returning to breathing mindfulness.

Humming

You have heard of Om, and have heard of Aum,
the sacred Hum of the throat as a drum,
the chakra sound that gives a man a voice and
puts him in the centre by aligning his frequency.

Humming is, therefore, the base sound,
the beginning of harmony, the beacon of
internal vibration, which is reverberating and
cleansing your body, your aura of toxicity.

Hum then, but speak no words,
hum then, but say no letters,
hum then, but create no sound,
hum now and count no breath.

Meditation

You should not stop meditating,
you should not start meditating,
you can not do meditation,
you can not meditate.

To meditate is to be,
to be is to meditate,
you can not change a thing,
what you should do is allow it to be.

You allow yourself then, your (true) self,
and by confiscating thoughts in the authority
of the inner peacefulness, the galloping echo of
the past and future will cease in your presence.

Breathing

That which is truly holy, which is truly sacred,
is neither a God in whom to believe and be faithful,
nor a priest, a healer, a shaman, but a
gradual to constant awareness of breathing.

When I say awareness, I mean conscious recognition,
by breathing, I mean the inner rhythm of God,
the natural ability to follow in and out
the essence of spirit that is alive inside us.

Consciousness, awareness, humming and meditation
will all support your recalibration towards
that sacred point of constancy, the deep breath in,
the long breath out, re-establishing peace as primary.

Inner Beauty

There is a person inside you,
the person of spiritual wisdom,
divine perceptibility, and eternal beauty,
emanating from the one source of knowledge.

If you think of yourself as a mischievous river
winding pointlessly through the world's wilderness,
you are about to realise that your particular inner
beauty is crucial for the very essence of life.

That person of inner knowing is your beauty,
the pure presence as awareness, and the
characteristic flavour of such perception is
the soul that dances with you in beingness.

Power of Awareness

Don't burden yourself with the future prize
of promised bliss, but reinvent yourself in the
now and all the pleasantness of being will manifest
of its own accord, with newfound liberation.

For a myriad has perished under the ingenuity of
ego, the ceaseless mind indulgence in delusions of
superiority, feeding off others' energy, whereas we
know those who are wise need only the Self.

Stay in peace, let the opinions drop away naturally,
let them cease in the presence of your being,
re-establish your power of awareness,
your inner clock is the moment's perseverance.

Soul

If you are not mentally free, how can you know the
self, a space of aware self is essential in recognising
beingness that is alive inside, to allow the peace
within, for the soul can only flourish in freedom.

Your soul is already well and alive, eager to be
expressed in acts of openness and selfness, that will
burst its banks like an ancient dam, overflowing
your fearful shyness and self-limiting smallness.

This beauty of the awakened universe and divine
softness exalt you in a heavenly oneness of
the long-forgotten self, thus once again inviting
the joy of aliveness, the essence of your soul.

Non-attachment

Without desire, wanting, or craving
nothing can possess you,
without possessions, nothing can own you,
without ownership, you are free.

To be unattached is the key to freedom,
to being free, to freeing the livelihood of the soul,
as in so doing you remain perfectly still,
unmoved, and untroubled by thoughts.

For that to which you attach you will have to carry
since you own it, and any burden, sad or pleasant
will have to be let go of, thus, without investments
in the world, you are truly liberated.

Freedom

Ah, the sweetest taste in life, the ability to choose,
welcome it open-handed and full-heartedly to guide
you towards an awakening of your truest self, to
manifesting a life of freedom and choice.

For this is your problem, you are trying to live
like this or that, inhibiting your freedom in doing so,
while returning to the knowing of presence would
awaken the truest wisdom which is your very soul.

Those who dare to forge a new way and liberate
the heart from an unconscious mind will truly find
the one infinite forever, as only in true being can
freedom rejoice within itself to live in aliveness.

Free Will

Relatively speaking, you have free will,
but, ultimately, looking at the totality of
the universal movement of happenings,
you are the destined awakening.

So you can choose this thing as
opposed to that thing, but finally,
consciousness chooses you to be
expressed as innermost awareness.

You need to let go of unconsciousness,
relax into consciousness, free your mind
and your ego from holding on to things
to experience the pure will of freedom.

Generality

Openness, vastness, space, consciousness,
in general, meaning freedom, transcendence and
comprehending existence in the fullest spectra
of expressing oneself in any given possibility.

Your witnessing of the world is a remarkable
phenomenon of being, as you know yourself as
a witness and your awareness of any and every
perception proves you are consciously aware.

In this overall understanding, you know everything,
you hold the door to knowing thyself, and within
that, you know everyone and everything else, as
generally, they encompass the same consciousness.

Authenticity

Who can you be if not yourself, as it's been said
"be yourself for everyone else is already taken,"
but how can you be yourself if you don't know who
or what you are: sacred presence and awareness.

By observing your unconscious, involuntary actions,
you will learn and know yourself as consciousness,
and from that state of peaceful being you will abide
and act in accordance with your own truest self.

That is the authenticity of yourself, the courage to live
based on this divine but most natural of intelligence,
unseparated from the very spark of life that sings
and dances in your fearlessly, openly shared heart.

Nowness

Throw away your worries about tomorrow,
forget your regrets about yesterday,
surrender fully and openly to the present day,
the presence of today, the moment's perseverance.

It is in this noticing of nowness that you will
find lasting happiness, that you will wake up to
the constancy of beingness and shining presentness,
the joy that is the self.

So open and full of itself, you abide in kindness,
rejoice in awareness, for in the absence of fear you
will discover yourself as the truest expression of the
now- moment, in ever-present satisfactoriness.

Who and What

What is within you
that has accompanied you
throughout your life,
a constant presence?

Who is it within you
that has remained the same,
guiding you through life,
the untouched spirit?

What is this you
that was always here
despite everything changing,
other than consciousness?

Truth

Whether it is telling the truth or
looking for the truth, there is rarely
anything more satisfying and
fulfilling for one's soul quest.

And the truth will set you free
if your being is wired to reality,
for only those who live in a fantasy
are incapable of being truthful.

What deeper, simpler or more
significant truth is there than the one
of your self-aware being, consciousness,
and the fact of being present, real and true?

BEING

Grace

A state of grace is upon you,
settling you with a merciful heart,
where you emanate unconditional kindness,
as the deepest expression of being.

In this tranquil state of compassion,
the wisdom of your authentic self is being
shared through an open channel of the one,
the centre as pure consciousness, pure love.

Now resting in the most liberating freedom,
in the space of no thought, no time, in peace,
radiating the power of the now, abiding in the
innermost wisdom and graceful beauty of being.

Compassion

The sense of oneness and shared being
between all God's creatures is compassion,
a glimpse into togetherness holds certainty
that tHere is only one consciousness.

THere is really no other there, just You in
an endless variety of existing, and feeling for
them is a sense of yourself, your true self, the self
that remains anchored in the unity of beings.

Call it oneness, love, brotherhood or sisterhood
of man, innermost beauty, deep open-hearted care,
so be it, feel it, awaken the sense of belonging to all,
passionately caring for the self in others.

Kindness

The most graceful of states is kindness,
the noblest of imperishable loves,
as you purify your mind with mercy,
kindness will cleanse you of all impurities.

Walk in this natural goodness of being and beauty
of feeling fearless and complete, be willing to
shine your authentic awakened flavour of
caring magnificence to those who flicker.

Your prize is already collected by the virtue of
the loving soul act, a senseless surrender to life
that spills its illuminating brilliance and fills
the whopping holes of unconsciousness.

Clarity

The only certainty we have in life is
the impermanence of all things, all things
shall pass, all creatures will die, all noise
will subside, all unconsciousness will cease.

Then perception is natural, sharp, momentary,
not clouded or delayed by the mind, thought or
feeling, but transparent through uncluttered
senses, through pure, crystal-clear consciousness.

This is your goal, your purpose in life, to attain
such a state, a promised bliss of egoless freedom,
a certainty in being as clear and clean as a perfectly
polished mirror where only the edges are distorted.

The Heart of Being

Make beingness your favourite subject,
invest everything into consciousness,
dedicate yourself to those in need,
create no further separation.

By divesting yourself of ego,
you abide in present mindfulness, and
in concentrating on your inner being, you walk
gracefully in each moment's pleasantness.

In silent solitude is where
the rest of you resides,
and in the very here,
your being rests in the now.

Divine Intellect

Outside time and space therein lies your
point of awareness, your divine intellect,
the present knowing centre you at the
heart of inner wisdom, the imperishable one.

In every moment it sleeps with the power
of agelessness and dreams of the eternal now,
an eternity in a moment, which is essentially
consciousness untouched by the mind.

It rests in spacelessness and abides in the
timelessness of infinitude, perceiving, observing,
continuously unmoved, being infinitely loved,
forever known and always feeling at home.

Inner Shrine of Wisdom

Within your being lies the power of immortality,
in the absence of thoughts, in the constancy of
beingness, only and ever in perfect stillness, in
the underlying attention of your natural existence.

The power is in not resisting what is, in observing
not complaining, for whoever is attentive enough to
the now, will abide in the absolute freedom of being,
beautiful silence and penetrating wisdom.

It is in those who manage to remain still
that the moment of salvation comes, it lingers and
flourishes exponentially, like riding an ever-increasing
wave of inner tranquillity, love and wisdom.

Spirit

Like an all-present God, feeling the entirety
of existence and truly knowing being, spirit
is everywhere and in everything, illuminating
and guiding the souls that are now awakening.

When you allow the present to be and let the force
of life be felt freely in your body's energy field, this
source of aliveness, spirit, will reverberate through
your soul & cells with the power of rejuvenation.

Keep that spirit alive, honour it like Christmas, create
the magic of life in song, food, art and well-being,
inspiring the community to be humble with ego
but proud in their hearts which makes them alive.

Being Present

Sit in perfect silence,
allow yourself stillness,
surrounded by darkness,
you are the consciousness.

As no time has passed,
and no place has changed,
you yourself have remained,
a motionless source of aliveness.

This place of no memories is
timeless beingness, it is the
place in space where
knowable is the self.

Knowing

Here you are again,
alone and perfectly still,
in the most familiar place,
knowing yourself as an eternal presence.

You know this is the point of inevitable return,
a true home of timeless belonging,
the perfect centre of inner peace
and universal knowing.

These are the deepest moments
that direct your life's interests,
which can always be reached through
a destined return to silence.

Peaceful

An inner state of stillness,
complete relaxed wakefulness,
in this penetrating silence,
remaining motionless.

You carry it forever alive inside,
abide in its nourishing kindness,
when all else seems restless,
be the light of its presence.

Peace is shown by being peaceful
not by an absence of deeds, where freedom
from thoughts in the heavenly ambience is
always within, as the light of your soul.

Silence

When you abide in presence, no words
are needed to describe this holy state,
the sole prerequisite is penetrating silence,
an eternal gaze, an awakening look of grace.

By this gesture of utmost presentness,
you initiate all those around you into
the journey of bliss and consciousness
by reawakening their inner stillness.

It is this transforming radiance that will
save humanity from damnation and hell,
by realising how all our problems stem
from the inability to be silent and still.

Death

Some cultures see it and embrace it
as the ultimate experience,
as a doorway to an after or eternal life,
while others try to ignore it.

But, as goes for you, I advise you
to know death by being around death
and know death by being alive yourself,
for whoever tastes a true life will be freed.

To know life, to accept death is to know your
innermost self as the constancy of awareness,
from where we all originate, before a thought
separates life from death again.

Exists tHere

You are right where you are, here and now,
and that place is the centre of your universe,
it is the event horizon of your existence,
here, and now, you are meant to be.

Therefore, to contemplate existence, start
from here, as in the innermost observation of time
and space, of others and the self, it turns out to be
the only place that exists and the only that tHere is.

You are existence, your own awareness of being
is self-evident proof that you are the one knowing
thoughts, the one who sees, the one who feels, and
the one aware of your own self-aware being.

Fundament

The fundamental reality, the absolute truth to
anything is complete silence, stillness, consciousness,
that is the being, a permeating and everlasting
presentness, that eternal, unchanging freshness.

Perhaps you know through intellect, realise it
through reason, or believe through virtue of faith,
religion or any spiritual or philosophical movement,
but by whatever means, you are correct.

But to feel it as yourself, as it is, and to be it, is
the greatest blessing that has arrived unto you, like
a spirit descending upon you, or the sweetest bliss of
being awakening as you, is the fundament of life.

Creation

The universe is the movement of mass & energy,
its swirling kinetics create objects like solar systems
bursting with stars and planets, which are
constantly birthing, changing and dying.

This matter is unconscious, unaware of its existence,
it comes, goes and changes form due to universal
laws, and you, as a soul in the human body, are
on a similar path of creation & destruction.

But tHere is a difference here, you are aware of this
process, you are consciousness, and she is never
created and can never be destroyed, she is never
born and will never die; you are your creation.

Universe

A tangible part of existence,
a huge space of scattered lights,
an enormous vacuum, void, ether, vast
emptiness paradoxically full of energy.

For humanity, me, and you
it is the greatest enigma,
one that makes us stand in awe,
fascinated but terrified to our chilled bones.

We are destined to develop and
consciously ponder the meaning of it all,
it is our essence to understand and comprehend,
to tap into, marvel and explore.

Existence

It is, literally, the greatest mystery in existence,
dual nature of non-dual reality, its infinity
drives scientists and philosophers to madness,
while providing bliss to those awakened.

We are a conscious part of an unconscious universe
and this relationship of awareness is accountable
for the knowing that we exist and that we
are both the source of existence.

Consciousness dreams itself as awareness,
and, as a side effect, existence is created as
a thinking, feeling, perceiving and knowing
phenomenon of being, a never-ending depth.

Oneness

We will all reunite with the one once
we surrender our bodies to the elements,
so let our souls roam free again,
liberated from both matter and ego.

In that moment of perfect presence,
the soul will fast realise its oneness with
the universe, and all the beings flying out
there will further surrender to the spirit.

Oneness is complete spirit, pure consciousness,
the non-dual self, perfection of existence,
singularity of God, total beingness,
unity of duality, unseparated, one.

Non-duality

To whom has this thought arisen,
to me,
who am I,
I AM THAT.

That Is,
It Is,
Is IS,
Isness.

The Self,
all,
not two,
one.

Beingness

Life is not a philosophy,
it is a being, a living experience,
it is not a figured-out state,
it is constant change.

Yet for the change to be possible,
for growth to be allowed to happen,
something eternal and unchanging must
be present, keeping existence grounded.

It is the centre of any & all movement,
the eye of anything that knows,
it encapsulates the entire universe,
anchors you in peace, no start, no finish.

I Am

I Am,
that I Am,
that, I Am,
I Am That.

We are,
together,
one,
not separate I Am's.

I Am we,
you are me,
I am you,
we I Am.

All Is Well

I feel so good just by being,
just by being alive and well,
as I sit peacefully right here and now,
having no resistance to the moment.

This is as good as it gets, just
being silently aware of surroundings,
just by patiently following all the senses,
what else would consciousness want?

There are no gods here, angels, at least
the ones we can't see, no ghosts or demons,
no aliens or spirits, there is only good
old raw, natural, pleasant observance.

The Art

Art is your particular unique style
of being present in the world,
the special way you abide
as consciousness, as awareness.

We each have a different taste to the soul,
a slightly differently flavoured spirit,
for it is in this multiplicity of beings
that we centre on our authenticity.

As you learn to be and manifest through
your expression of being by openly sharing it,
awesome goodness will radiate in your
freed awakened Being.

*"Your soul is a beautiful, radiant light
with a twelve-petal lotus in its centre.
As you evolve, the petals unfold to
reveal a radiant jewel in the centre.
This is the light of Spirit,
the essence of your being.*

*Seven rays of beautiful colour come
out of the jewel, adding all the qualities
of the soul to every part of your being.
Your soul sends streams of mental, emotional
and physical energy into your chakras.
These streams of energy create the 'you',
forming your personality, thoughts,
feelings and physical body.*

*The solar light shines upon your soul
all the way down to the physical plane,
lifting all life upward to return home,
to live permanently in the higher
realms of Light and Love."*

Chapter II

the Joy
of
Living

Loving

Love

The world is bathed in songs, books, movies, arts, teachings and preachings, adorned with stereotypes and promises of salvation, the eternal happiness of feeling complete with the other, in love, forever.

Have you felt it, have you experienced it, have you been in love, have you reaped the fruits of the promised harvest of endless, constant joy and happiness, or have you fallen from grace instead?

Don't seek love, you can only give it without expecting anything in return, and in that very act, feeling the love you are freely sharing, is an instant reward for the unselfish heart.

Romance

To be romantic means to care, to
have an open heart, to be willing to
share your soul, to have a style and
to enjoy others' special happiness.

Romance is magic you create with
that one person you appreciate, not
just adorned with candles and roses, but
freely uniting your two hearts of gold.

To be romantic means to love,
to fulfil each other's lives with well-being
and purpose, to prolong society with
the children you've grown.

Community

No human, animal or creature has ever sprung out
without parents, without a community, tribe, nation
or civilisation, all biological & spiritual beings come
from other beings, we are, by birth, all socialist.

So how have we ended up right here & now, in this
time & place, living largely individual destinies,
where many of our 8 billion friends don't even
have husbands or wives, never mind children?

If the cause is density, scarcity, prices or our strong
senses of individuality, the solution would be to start
a thriving community of intelligible, loving families,
whose children will heal the earth itself.

Family

Soul love — your partner's joy,
playing time — children's happiness,
utmost dedication — family's well-being,
quality relations — relatives' peace.

Your family is your creation, your honour,
your pride, your responsibility, your joy,
your contribution, your home, your priority,
your will, purpose and inspiration.

They are your life, love, blessing,
gratitude, your genes, pleasure, satisfaction,
your constant engagement, your fun, your
livelihood, your greatest gift from God.

Human being

People tend to feel superior and
abuse the system as soon as they taste
even moderate success, which, more often
than not, leads to crime and punishment.

They look down on people who are poor or
just have less, as they measure everything by
its value on the market, but, above all, human
beings seek for one thing, they want happiness.

It's true to say, some just want peace of mind, so
however we look at all our fellow human beings,
we must stay true to ourselves and our soul virtues,
then wealth will be opportune to share.

Giving & Sharing

The idea of ownership is based on scarcity and an inflated sense of personal belonging, both are facets of ego, but what if you had everything you need, would you still care for possessing and holding on to things?

Now imagine if everything was free, by having plenty it would be easy to share, such an act wouldn't take a second thought, perhaps there wouldn't even be any need as everyone would already be provided for.

To give is to give from your heart, your labour, your sweat and tears, knowing that this gesture of unconditional love has far-reaching consequences for the individual in need, ergo for humanity entirely.

Business

To be an entrepreneur, be a leader, give respect, invest in innovation, and, above all, create a community of happy, well-rewarded workers, consequently, you benefit and a thriving business is guaranteed.

Get to know them, earn their trust, be their friend, oppose standard practice by creating emotional bonds, help them feel they are working on their progress and career, not just for the business.

It's all about connection, moving forwards, inspiration from new exciting projects and quality service, integrated with life, making your career the highest excitement, and you will never work again.

Intuition

Everybody says to follow your intuition so
there must be some element of truth in this as
I think nobody has ever regretted following it,
but what it truly is, perhaps nobody knows yet.

It might be a sense of the same life that has already
happened, a déjà-vu moment of a particular time &
space, the innermost calling of the heart and the soul
leading you towards your destined return to self.

The truth is simple, intuition is your natural sense,
inborn guidance towards achieving well-being, joy,
and happiness, it is your soul's investment into a
livelihood, you just need to be it, as you are life itself.

Creativity

It could be your greatest asset, this talent of creativity,
fulfilling your life with endless possibilities of
inspiration, producing goods that will surely benefit
humanity, a lifetime achievement of joyousness.

But never think of it as an innate gift you are born
with, rather, liberate your being, clear your mind and
open your heart from any and such limitations and
creative art will start flowing like an endless river.

Tap into this all-present and everlasting stream of
inspired precrastination by releasing yourself from
indoctrinated dogmas, for you are an all-powerful
being, so fly in an open sky, free from perplexity.

Science

Development serving knowledge,
understanding the world of large & small,
correcting superstitions, laying her to rest,
discovering equations of the laws.

You can study any of her many branches,
looking deeply into nature, feeling her soul,
touching God by comprehending the
intricacy of the forces.

As an investment into humanity's
prosperous and sustainable future,
we must secure the funds and
educate ourselves in all the sciences.

Natural Sense

Why trouble your mind with fantasies,
why obsess over superstitions, why live
in fear of beliefs, when the only thing you
can ever really notice is the raw nature of reality.

Don't be afraid to remain still, using your
reason and your senses to observe what is now,
what is here and what truly does matter
to the essence of your being.

I advise you now to sit down and meditate, don't
be afraid to abandon tradition, try something else or
experiment, for the only thing you will discover tHere
is more of who you are, don't just believe me, try it.

Exercise & Sport

We knew of sports games ever since we knew
of civilisation, it is the basis of entertainment
and leisure time since it uses the body,
one of the cornerstones in this life.

Exercise is about health, sport is about fun
and both are a passion for feeling well & alive,
so indulge in it, learn the movements and feel
the body as a physical extension of yourself.

Make it a healthy foundation for life's challenges
and you will only find them fun to deal with,
so go and play with precision, heartiness, strength
and endurance, and breathing in full lungs of air.

Far & Wide

Being able to find your way in time
and space, in distance and place,
it must be the most original and
adventurous feeling a human can have.

To witness the world for the first time,
to see new horizons and meet different cultures,
to engage your entire waking day in the present
moment of discovering new ways and landscapes.

This is where the human spirit feels most alive,
but only if it is based on the useful purpose of
broadening the senses and sharing that
awakened happiness with all who care.

Self-Sustenance

The biological body thrives on organic cells,
fresh stream water, minerals and vitamins,
so your job is to allow for this abundance of
environmental wilderness, permaculture its name.

The good way to start is your back garden, fill it
with herbs, flowers, fruits & veggies, trees, compost
and from there you start investing in your
livelihood and sustenance, your sustainable self.

If you live in a city or don't yet have a garden,
what option do you have but to dedicate all your
remaining efforts to moving somewhere else with
enough provided land to live, eat, be healthy & free.

Hobby

Life is an opportunity to feel and experience,
to learn, share and enjoy, so it is wise to have
some interests or hobbies because what you
do with your spare time, matters the most.

I would recommend feeling into what you like,
what excites you, what you are good at and
love to enjoy, such as playing music or
sport, creating art, fixing or building.

Maybe you are even lucky enough to learn and
graduate with your passion in school, in college,
and evolve your hobbies into a career,
to life, to the bliss of your soul.

Reading

Once you find yourself in the truth of eternal
presence, your life will never be the same again, and
you will want to preserve that experience, that special
moment of inner wisdom and illuminating radiance.

Start by writing it down, talk about it to friends
and share it with others, but, for the majority, it
means you will start looking for it outside of yourself
and for that, you will start to read everything.

By reading, you can confirm what you already
know to be true in yourself, recognise the similarity
and the sameness of experience and preserve the
miracle in books you have accumulated.

Writing

It has been and remains the most important base
of civilised society, most of what we do and know
comes in written format as artefacts, scrolls,
bibles, sciences, laws, proclamations, books...

Everything started in written form, as diagrams,
equations, notes, lyrics, ideas or scripts, as
fingerprints and footprints of understanding,
teachings, entertainment and knowledge sharing.

There is no great excuse not to write for yourself
or something of significance for others, to open up
your soul's knowledge and record it on paper,
with all inventions, only writing forever remains.

Singing

There are some inherent behavioural traits
embedded in man, the ability and need to sing
or vocalise is one of them and there is evidence
this was also true for ancient, tribal man.

And as they freely sang expressing their feelings
naturally from spirit, the modern human has
expanded on singing by making it into an art
to listen to, a gift to have and a talent to train.

And as with everything else today, he puts a price
tag on the voice, on performance, that attracted many
seeking out fortune and fame, meanwhile discour-
aging everyone else, but you sing regardless.

Music

Oh, what joy music brought to humanity through
the ages, performing the sounds of the soul,
dancing our hearts in countless celebrations,
accompanying both the lonely and joyous,
healing the heart, curing us all.

And those artists, musicians, singers, teachers,
conductors and performers, those with a gift, the
talent, will, courage and love to create, perform, sing
and preserve, what glory goes to them, all of it.

There is not a human being who is not touched or
moved by music, it is a vibration in us all, and you
too, if not already, can play, dance, sing and record
the sounds of your mind, heart and soul.

Animals

They have no self-awareness yet
they behave socially like humans,
they have no grasp of the earth
yet they are an intrinsic part of it.

Animals could never know the universe
yet we project them as star constellations,
they could never be the same as us yet
we've domesticated them as pets for life.

And yet we abuse them on a planetary level,
caging, killing and eating in their billions,
destroying their natural habitat, ploughing it so
they can never return, but you can be alternative.

Travel

If I could agree with only one saying
that has accompanied my experience,
it would be *to travel is to live*,
for travel is the being itself.

To witness something for the first
time is a constant feeling of beingness,
just the excitement of it is bliss
and being on the journey is true heaven.

Travel is a feeling of perceiving the world,
cultures, history and space, so many different
people, but wait a moment, they're all decent
humans, just like you and me, all the same.

Food

We could live off the sun's energy,
but until then we'll have to deal with food,
which is not so bad, after thousands of years
we have become experts in taste.

Food is an energy source to power your
muscles, to grow, heal and maintain the tissue,
but spice it up with a delectable flavour to
make it feel, look and taste even better.

In truth, food should be our joy, as some cultures
already know, they have learnt to eat and enjoy with
the blessed feeling of thankfulness, but don't ever let
food eat you, remember you are the one eating food.

Juicing

By distilling the raw essence of fruits, herbs and
veggies, you are extracting the purely natural source
of minerals, fibre and vitamins, which will hit
you exactly where you need it the most.

This organic, fresh, natural supplement is the
superfood of the day, the moment you taste it, you
feel the nourishment of your being, empowering
your living essence to the point of uncontrollable joy.

This much-needed, vital energy source derived
of the sun's light is the colourful fluid link essential
in building the body and maintaining a healthy
connection to your soul, your spirit.

Spirituality

Health

By all means, it is the most important of gifts,
the greatest blessing from God, the most natural
of living rights, the one we should
take care of much, much more.

It does not mean obsessing over yourself,
your diet and your exercises, for the majority,
it only means stopping harming your
mental and physical well-being.

You can be hungry, you can be poor,
but if you are sick, what chance is there at all,
the sick want only to recover, to be well, you
hold the knowledge inside as the middle way.

Nature

Biological extension of consciousness,
thriving, organic, evolutionary aliveness,
the most natural circle of life and death,
but nobody is aware of it, nobody is there.

Nature is a program, self-replicated,
it does not know it exists, yet it lives,
you are a conscious extension of her,
neither separated nor alone, but awareness.

Cherish nature, your basic necessity for existence,
as it provides you with your every need to eat and
breathe, nourishing your body with nutrients,
you are her guardian, her spirit.

Camping

Allow yourself the freedom to go out to nature for
a couple of days, refrain from carrying any mental
baggage, take no worldly problems, no stress
and go where no noise can follow you.

Choose that one special place with an open
space that is reminiscent of a natural living room,
set out your tent, sit under the sun close to a stream
enjoying the freedom of the freshest moments.

In this authentic serenity you don't have to think
about tomorrow, you don't remember yesterday, for
the fish in the water are as carefree as the bird on
the branch or a bee in the field, you are awareness.

Sunshine

Is there anything more life inspiring
than the very warmth of the radiant sun,
embracing you with its natural light
and its energetic healing properties?

Whenever you have the chance, take a
moment to stop and relax in front of this
luminous sunshine, feel the heat on your
closed eyes, return to home in the sky.

Revel in this experience to the point of bliss,
carry that spark, that flame of the burning
sun inside, combine it with a natural ambience
and even arrange your life according to it.

Wonderful is Life

For the very fact you exist wonderful is life,
in every moment of your day, life is a wonder
because life starts with you, through your eyes
and the perceptions of your consciousness.

How beautiful life is with your existence,
every day wakes up for you and sleeps in you,
the sun shines brightly for you, sending you
vitality with its brilliant life-giving energy.

Isn't life fantastic by having you here, enabling
your fully aware being, giving the privilege
of your graceful state of universal existence,
wonderful is life for being just as you are.

Volunteering

To give your free time, your effort or wealth,
to give yourself to a common cause that betters
others without expecting anything in return, just
to help is to better yourself on the deepest level.

To be selfless, to sacrifice yourself, to give and
invest your energy in a goal that benefits
humanity, to work for another human being,
for animals and the planet is to awaken.

For it is exactly this unselfish volunteering
practice that unites the heart in feeling
united, unseparated, as one, when it comes
to the human spirit, life so sacred.

Religion

A mass celebration of one's holiness,
some say it is opium for the masses,
but it is a spiritual community of devotees,
those who remain humble but want to be free.

It is a sacred worship of practising peace with
yourself so that you can remain in peace with others,
for in another you are acknowledging your own
divine self, the timeless teacher it remains.

When it arises from control, religion is a suppression
of diversity, but if derived from the heart, it is the
preservation of eternal truth, the flourishing of art,
organised recognition of love and shared happiness.

Devotion

To devote is to honour your deepest self in others,
to respect and show adoration to others is to recognise
awakened qualities that you cherish within yourself,
and to serve is to humbly show your own greatness.

Be a devotee to progress in melting away your ego,
in the sweetest bliss of life nurture your awakening,
be devoted to love unconditionally offered to
others since it knows no separation.

In such an absence of duality, in the presence
of the self, the dividing line disappears between
devotees and those receiving such devotion as they
experience the conundrum of the one beingness.

Home Shrine

Build your own shrine at home,
in a special place, in a special corner,
put into it your deepest devotion, your best art,
everything that presents your holiest now.

And be truly devoted to it,
like it is God itself emanating there,
with all the grace, power, heart, love, emotion,
the unity of yourself, you & self, that is God.

This shire is your doorway to God, to self, where
the burning scents are a heavenly invitation into the
sacredness of your being, the holiest blessing, and
the presentation of shining, awakened awareness.

God

Trust me or not, God is not a person, or
some deity in heaven or in the sky, for you
are the supreme authority of your life and
God is an inseparable part of who we are.

To know God, one has to know oneself,
to know yourself one has to know thyself,
to know thyself one has to abide in grace,
to abide in grace is to see God's face.

So be it, God is the one consciousness,
a deathless spirit, while your essence is infinite,
timeless, spaceless, unconditional love,
and by being, all glory goes to God.

Teacher

Every soul needs a teacher
if no other than his own self,
but, the rest of us, we depend
on their shared love and wisdom.

Whether Pope, Dalai Lama, Muhammad,
Rupert Spira, or Eckhart Tolle,
by all means, any of the greats,
learn from their experience.

A true teacher is no teacher,
but they will settle you in peace,
and invoke your true being,
as for the rest goes, suffer unto me.

Jesus

Is love,
Christ consciousness,
blissful,
all-seeing.

He is on the mission
of human salvation,
in one God,
in unconditional love.

Allow yourself
to melt in his heart,
and open the door
to eternal life.

Buddha

Is wisdom,
Buddha nature,
wise,
all-knowing.

He is on a mission
of human enlightenment,
in true awakening,
in the middle way.

Allow yourself
to concentrate on his stillness,
and in quieting the mind, enjoy
bliss in transcendence.

Ramana

Is peace,
a liberated being,
self-abiding,
all-present.

He is on the mission
of human self-inquiry,
in perfect attention,
in penetrating silence.

Allow yourself
to remain peaceful in his gaze,
and flood your being with
unalloyed happiness.

Awakening

To sleep is to be in a mind domain,
to awaken means to be present,
to be present is to control the ego,
and to be in control is consciousness.

Awakening is the regaining of the sense
of awareness by which one is capable of
remaining observant without interrupting
the natural flow of presence.

It is not some miraculous acquisition
of spiritual powers, but the simplest
ability to notice what is, and this
is the universe looking at itself.

Living

You are the universe made aware,
you wear the universe in every atom,
this essence of stars and spaciousness is
your universal shine on the earth's surface.

You have a body to carry your awareness on
the journey of feeling universality, and
your waking perception provides the
joy of unfathomable realisations.

Just to be alive like that, like this, like
you are in and being part of everything,
is enough to already be at home in your heart
and living the joy that accompanies you always.

Innermost

Do you finally feel so light
as only true freedom can be,
do you feel in your heart so
much wisdom, so much peace?

All the knowledge in the world starts
with you, it is in you, and it is meant to
be shared to create the knowledge of
the world, of self, the essence divine.

This is authentic spiritual freedom,
the one all the teachers pointed to,
is knowing yourself as awareness,
awakening an innermost expression of being.

Bliss

Your freed mind,
your awakened heart,
is the soul blissful,
your natural self.

Your authenticity,
pure consciousness,
is the bliss of
your being.

Your fearless state,
your imperishable grace,
is the joy blissful of
inner love.

Joy

Once you perceive the world without a thought,
the joy of your natural being will shine forth,
so you only need to do the work of staying still,
engaging with the heart, and having no fear.

How hard can that be, staying true to your
natural self as opposed to playing roles of
being something that you're not,
filling in the societal norms and forms?

You are one unique expression of God
manifested as the universe, with the ability
to experience itself as the joy of each
and every being, existing to enjoy.

Peace

When you wake up, lay in peace,
go to the bathroom and brush your teeth,
then after eating something light
return to bed and meditate in peace.

Go out to the park, walk, sit, read in peace,
stay in the sun, take full deep breaths,
feel alive and awaken your inner being,
bliss and fortune, remaining still in peace.

Upon returning home, do something in peace,
be creative in writing, cooking, be artsy,
and when doing is done, surrender to
being, in the silent moment, in peace.

Happiness

All humans desire
one above all,
to be joyous,
to be happy.

Happiness is
therefore everyone's
natural right, *it is not
wrong to desire it.*

*What is wrong is seeking it
outside when it is inside,*
as the Joy of your
BEING.

Petar Umiljanović,

was born in Croatia on the 28th of June 1987.

From an early age, He felt strangely connected to and interested in the Universe, Nature, Religion, and Mysteries, along with Science, History, Ufology, Sport, and Music.

Later, profound insights into Psychology, Philosophy, and Spirituality led Him to investigate the True nature of the Self, revealing Consciousness as the only constant Presence.

Upon moving to Ireland and travelling Europe, thus engaging in many arts and activities, especially experiencing a deep relationship with Nature, this book was gradually inspired.

Contact:
petarumiljanovic@gmail.com

Notes

Notes

Printed in Great Britain
by Amazon

19045019R00079